GEOGRAPHY FILES

Rivers

Gianna Williams

WAYLAND

GEOGRAPHY FILES

First published in 2007
by Wayland
This book is based on *Geography Fact Files: Rivers* by Mandy Ross originally published by Wayland.

Wayland
338 Euston Road
London NW1 3BH

Wayland Australia
Hachette Children's Books
Level 17/207 Kent Street
Sydney, NSW 2000

Produced by Discovery Books

Subject consultant: Keith Lye

Illustrations: Michael Posen

British Library Cataloguing Publication Data
Williams, Gianna

Rivers. - (Geography files)
1. Rivers - Juvenile literature
I. Title
551.4'83

ISBN-13: 978 07502 5268 3

Printed in China.

Wayland is a division of Hachette Children's Books

Acknowledgements

We are grateful to the following for permission to reproduce photographs: Aerofilms.com 17 bottom; Associated Press 11 bottom (Apichart Weera Wong); Corbis back cover bottom (Ales Fevzer), 13 bottom (Hulton-Deutsch), 27 (Kevin Fleming), 42 (Ales Fevzer); Digital Vision 47; Ecoscene 41 (Stephen Coyne); FLPA 6 (Minden Pictures), 29 bottom (David Hosking), 37 top (Skylight); Getty images front cover (Jeremy Woodhouse); Nature Picture Library 10 (Pete Oxford), 19 (Paul N Johnson), 21 top (A and S Chandola), 23 top (Vincent Munier), 24 (John Cancalosi), 28 (Staffan Widstrand), 40 top (Jean Roche); NHPA 4 (David Woodfall), 18 (NASA/ T&T Stack), 20 (David Woodfall), 40 bottom (David Woodfall); Edward Parker 25; Popperfoto 38, 39 (Juda Ngwenya/Reuters); Robert Harding Picture Library 3 middle (T Waltham), 3 bottom (Paul Allen), 5 bottom (Roy Rainford), 9, 11 top, 14, 15 (T Waltham), 22 (Paul Allen), 23 bottom (Gary Schultz), 29 top (Gavin Hellier); Science Photo Library 36 (Martin Bond); Still Pictures 1 (S J Krasemann), 3 top (BAV/Helga Lade GmbH), 5 top (BAV/Helga Lade GmbH), 17 top (S J Krasemann), 26 (Hartmut Schwarzbach), 33 bottom (Jorgen Schytte), 35 (Jim Wark), 37 bottom (Michael Coupard), 43 (J Sackermann/Das Fotoarchiv), 44 (Uniphoto International); Topham Picturepoint 13 top (Rob Crandall/Image Works), 21 bottom (Tom Brakefield/ Image Works), 30 (Jim Pickerell/Image Works), 31 (Lee Snider/Image Works), 32 (Owen Humphreys/PA), 46 (Lee Snider/Image Works); WaterAid 45 (Jon Spaull).

Contents

The words that are explained in the glossary are printed in **bold**.

What is a river?

A river is a large stream of fresh water. Rivers start high in the mountains as small streams. Most rivers end when they reach the sea. Rivers are important because living things need water.

◄ Most streams begin high in the mountains, like this one in Wales.

There are rivers all over the world. Rivers flow through cold areas, through **tropical** rain forests and through deserts. Many cities are built on the banks of great rivers.

Life would be hard without rivers. They provide food and water. Rivers are a useful way of travelling and they are popular places for holidays. But rivers can be dangerous, for example when they flood, or when they are polluted.

Fact file

River facts

- The world's longest river is the River Nile in Africa. It is about 6,650 km long.
- The Roe River in Montana, USA, is one of the world's shortest rivers. It is about as long as 15 cars!
- Rivers make up only a tiny fraction of the world's fresh water – just 0.003 per cent.

The Mississippi River

The name Mississippi means 'big river' in Algonkian, a Native American language. The Mississippi-Missouri River starts as a stream. Many rivers join it along its 5,971 km course. In places it is nearly two kilometres wide. The Mississippi is one of the busiest rivers in the world.

◀ **The Mississippi passes through 10 US states.**

▼ **Many great cities have grown up at a river crossing, such as Paris, France, on the River Seine.**

Rivers have to be treated carefully, because what is done to a river in one place may affect it further down.

Rivers and the water cycle

The same water on Earth is constantly changing form. This is called the water cycle. Rivers are a part of the water cycle. The water in rivers flows into the ocean. There the water **evaporates**, forms clouds and later falls as rain. So the whole cycle starts again.

Great rivers

Some of the world's great rivers are thousands of kilometres long. Some are so wide that if you stand on one bank, you can't see the other side. So which is the world's greatest river?

There are many ways of measuring a river. One way is to measure its length. Rivers bend and curve, so the measurement has to follow all the curves.

Another way of comparing the size of rivers is to measure the amount of water in them. Yet another way is to measure the area of land that feeds rainwater into the river. This total area is called a river's **basin**.

▶ In places, the River Amazon is 10 km wide.

Fact file

The world's longest rivers

River	Destination	Length (km)
Nile	Mediterranean Sea	6,650
Amazon-Ucayali-Apurimac	South Atlantic Ocean	6,400
Yangtze (Chang Jiang)	East China Sea	6,300
Mississippi-Missouri-Red Rock	Gulf of Mexico	5,971
Ob-Irtysh	Gulf of Ob	5,410
Yellow River (Huang He)	East China Sea	4,672
Yenisey-Baikal-Selenga	Kara Sea	4,093
Parana	South Atlantic Ocean	3,999

Fact file

Rivers with the largest basin

River	Location	Basin (km²)
Amazon	South America	7,180,000
Congo	Africa	3,822,000
Nile	Africa	3,349,000
Mississippi-Missouri	North America	3,221,000
Ob	Siberia	2,975,000
Parana	S. America	2,650,000
Yenisey-Angara	Siberia	2,605,000
Lena	Asia	2,490,000
Niger	Africa	1,500,000

The Amazon is only the second-longest river in the world, but it has the most water. This is because the Amazon has the biggest basin. Most of the rivers of the northern half of South America flow into the Amazon. About one-fifth of all the world's river water flows out of the Amazon into the Atlantic Ocean!

▼ This map shows the world's greatest rivers.

Springs and sources

Where do rivers start? Many of the world's great rivers start as tiny streams in high mountains. For instance the source of the River Ganges, in Asia, is high in the Himalayan mountains.

High in the mountains there is a lot of rain and snow. The rain runs quickly down the steep slopes into streams. These streams join together to form a river.

Rivers are also fed by mountain snow and ice that melt in summer. If the weather warms up quickly, melting a lot of snow, rivers can suddenly get much deeper, and sometimes flood.

People file

Who found the Nile source?

The River Nile has two main **sources**, the Blue Nile and the White Nile. The first European to see the source of the Blue Nile was the Spaniard Father Pedro Páez in 1618. In 1937 a German explorer, Dr. Burkhart Waldecker, traced the source of the White Nile to the state of Burundi. A small pyramid there now marks Waldecker's discovery.

▼ The making of a river.

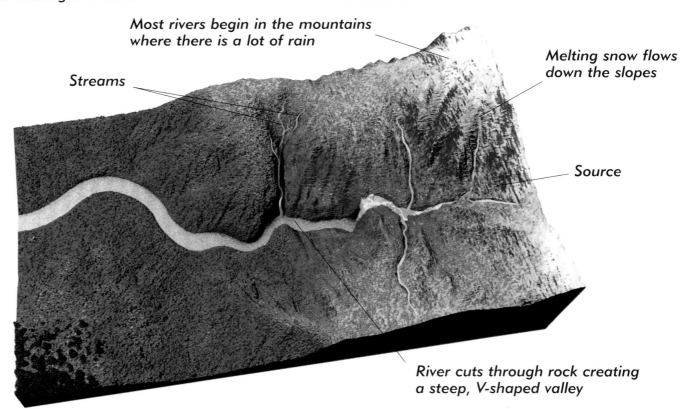

Most rivers begin in the mountains where there is a lot of rain

Streams

Melting snow flows down the slopes

Source

River cuts through rock creating a steep, V-shaped valley

Other rivers start from a source called a **spring**. Rainwater trickles through rocks, then flows underground until it comes out again at a spring.

On low ground, water sometimes gathers in pools, or sits on the surface. This is known as a bog, marsh or swamp. Water trickles out of bogs into streams and rivers.

The Rhine and Rhône

Two of Europe's great rivers, the Rhine (above) and the Rhône, begin from sources close together in the Swiss Alps, but they flow out in opposite directions. The Rhine flows 1,390 km north and west across the Netherlands into the North Sea. The 813 km-long Rhône flows south through France and out into the Mediterranean Sea.

▲ **Barges** on the River Rhine carrying goods.

Down the mountain

As rivers flow they loosen rocks and soil. They may carry along large boulders and lots of mud, sometimes all the way to the sea. The water crushes the rocks into smaller pieces. They end up as tiny grains of sand called **sediment**. Soil is washed into rivers by rain. Every stream that joins a river brings some sediment with it.

Sediment

When a river flows quickly, sediment is carried along in the water. When the water slows down, the sediment can fall to the bottom of the river. This clogs up the river and makes it dangerous for ships sailing along it.

Some sediment is carried all the way to the sea. In Asia, the Ganges, Yellow River and Brahmaputra carry one-fifth of the world's sediment into the sea.

▼ The water of a tributary flowing into the Amazon is a different colour because its sediment is made from a different soil.

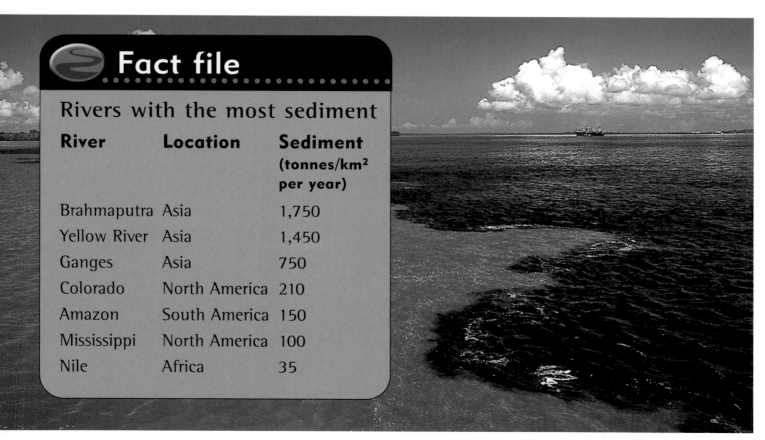

Fact file

Rivers with the most sediment

River	Location	Sediment (tonnes/km² per year)
Brahmaputra	Asia	1,750
Yellow River	Asia	1,450
Ganges	Asia	750
Colorado	North America	210
Amazon	South America	150
Mississippi	North America	100
Nile	Africa	35

▲ Forests, like this one in South Africa, are often cut down either for their wood, or to clear land for farming and buildings.

Forests – or floods?

Cutting down trees can damage nearby rivers. Tree roots help to keep soil from washing into a river when it rains. Trees and plants soak up rainwater, which helps to stop floods. When forests are cut down, floods become more common.

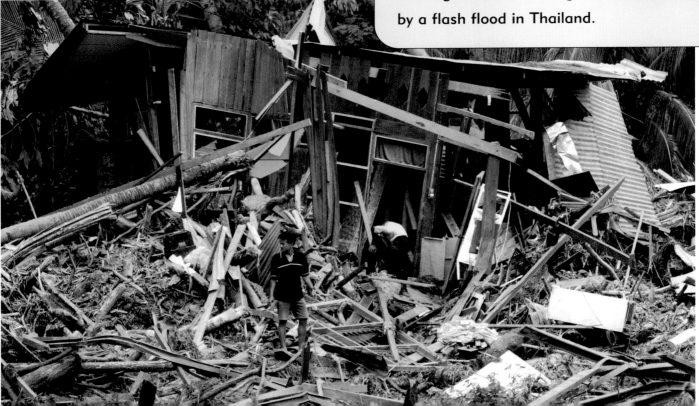

Valleys and waterfalls

River valleys are being formed all the time. Rivers can carve deep valleys and plunging waterfalls.

Valleys

Stones and gravel in the water grind down a river's **bed**, carving a narrow V-shaped path.

Glaciers are large rivers of ice that carve valleys as they slide towards the sea. Glaciers make a wide U-shaped valley. The longest glacier in the world is in the Antarctic. It is 515 km long.

Some river valleys, called wadis, run through deserts. They are usually dry because wadis were formed thousands of years ago, when there was enough rain to let rivers flow there. Today wadis are only ever filled if unusual amounts of rain cause a flash flood.

▶ The action of a river carves a V-shaped valley.

◀ The action of a glacier carves a U-shaped valley.

Fact file

Waterfalls

- The world's highest waterfall – Angel Falls (right), on the River Churun in Venezuela, South America – drops 979 m.
- The widest waterfall is the Khon Cataracts in Laos, Asia. It is over 10 km wide!
- The waterfall with the most water is the Boyoma Falls in the Democratic Republic of Congo, Africa.

Waterfalls and rapids

A waterfall is a place where a river drops over a cliff. Many waterfalls are formed when a river flows over different kinds of rock. The water wears away soft rock over thousands of years, and leaves a cliff of hard rock.

Rapids are places where a river races along a steep slope. Rapids form when the rock is too hard for the river to wear it down.

▲ Angel Falls in Venezuela is the world's highest waterfall.

People file

Blondin

In 1859, the French acrobat Jean-Francois Gravelet (1824-1897), known as Blondin, crossed the Niagara gorge, between the USA and Canada, on a tightrope. He crossed many times, backwards, blindfolded, and once sitting down halfway to cook and eat an omelette!

◄ Blondin crosses the Niagara River on a tightrope.

Gorges, canyons, caves

Canyons and gorges are steep valleys where a river has cut deep into the rock. Many caves are also formed by rivers, where the water flows underground.

Canyons can be as small as a narrow crack or as big as an enormous trench. A river flows at the bottom, constantly carving away at the rock.

The Grand Canyon in the USA is the world's deepest, longest and widest canyon. It was carved out by the Colorado River. Down its sides, the Grand Canyon has layers of rock. The oldest rocks are two billion years old.

 Fact file

Deep down
- The Grand Canyon (right) is 446 km long and its walls are up to 1,737 m deep. At its widest point, the canyon is 29 km wide.
- The deepest river in the world is China's Yangtze River, where it runs through the Three Gorges. Here the river is 180 m deep.

▶ The rocks at the bottom of the Grand Canyon date from around 2 billion years ago. Those at the top are about 250 million years old.

Caves and potholes

Sometimes water seeps through rock and flows underground, along cracks in the rock. As more water flows through the cracks, they get wider. The water forms an underground river, which in time can carve out a cave.

Exploring caves, or potholing, is a popular hobby. Potholers squeeze through narrow cracks to find new caves. Potholing can be dangerous, especially if the water level rises after unexpected heavy rain.

▲ An underground river wore away the Clearwater Cave, above, in Mulu National Park, Malaysia.

 **Location file**

Mammoth cave

The Mammoth Cave National Park and the Flint Ridge Cave System in Kentucky, USA, make up a long network of underground caves, rivers and lakes. Over 50 types of animals have been found there, including blind fish and colourless spiders.

Meanders and lakes

1n the mountains, a river travels fast down steep slopes. Once it reaches lower land, it slows down. Lakes form when a river flows into a low area of land.

Meanders

The loops and curves of a slow-moving river are called **meanders**. Meanders have a curved shape because the water flows faster around the outer edge of the loop, and over time widens it.

Sometimes when the river is high or floods, it cuts across a meander and makes a straighter path. This can leave a lake called an oxbow lake. Oxbow lakes fill up with soil and plants, and become bogs.

Fact file

World's largest lakes

Lake	Location	Area (km²)
Caspian Sea	Asia	386,400
Lake Superior	North America	82,100
Lake Victoria	Africa	69,485
Lake Huron	North America	59,600
Lake Michigan	North America	57,800
Lake Tanganyika	Africa	32,900
Lake Baikal	Siberia	31,500
Aral Sea	Asia	17,160

▼ This diagram shows how a river meanders.

Sediment collects on the inner edge of the meander

The river flows fastest around the outer edge of the meander

Sometimes the river cuts across the meander. With no water flowing in or out, sediment collects at the entrance and exit and they close up, forming an oxbow lake.

▶ The amazing twists and turns of a meandering river in Alaska, USA. You can see an oxbow lake in the centre of the picture.

Lakes

Lakes are formed when a river flows through a hollow in the ground, or when the river is blocked. Water fills up the hollow. Sometimes a stream or river flows out of the lowest edge of the lake. In some cases, such as Australia's Lake Eyre, these lakes can become salty. Some lakes are so large they are called seas.

 Location file

Shrewsbury

The historic town of Shrewsbury (right), on the border between England and Wales, was built inside a loop of the River Severn. It was built there because the river protected the town from invaders during the **Middle Ages**.

▶ **This aerial view of Shrewsbury shows how the old town was surrounded by the river.**

The river's mouth

A river ends when it joins with another river, or ends up in the sea or in a lake. This place is called the river's **mouth.**

Almost all rivers end up in the sea or the ocean. There are a few exceptions. The River Volga in Russia actually flows into the world's largest lake, the Caspian Sea. Many rivers meet the sea with such force that they keep flowing for several kilometres into the sea. The Amazon River flows out into the sea for 160 km!

▼ A view of the Yangtze River from space shows its muddy water emptying into the sea.

Fact file

Rivers with the most water at river mouth
(m^3 of water per second)

River	Location	Water
Amazon	South America	180,000
Congo	Africa	42,000
Yangtze	China	35,000
Orinoco	South America	28,000
Brahmaputra	Asia	20,000
Yenisey-Angara	Siberia	19,600
Parana	South America	19,500
Mississippi	North America	17,545

Location file

The Wash

In Norfolk, England, the River Ouse opens into a great estuary called the Wash (above). It is one of Europe's richest wildlife **habitats**. Huge flocks of ducks, geese and other birds from the Arctic spend the winter there. In the summer, birds such as lapwings breed in the estuary.

▲ Flocks of birds on a river estuary in Norfolk, UK.

Estuaries

Most rivers grow wider as they approach the sea. This wider area at the river's mouth is called an **estuary**. Here river water meets sea water.

A river slows down when it reaches the estuary. The sediment in its water settles on the bottom and along its banks. When the tide goes out, this river mud is left behind. These areas are called **mudflats**. Mudflats are rich feeding grounds for many birds. They dig with their beaks for creatures under the mud.

19

Deltas and swamps

When a river meets the sea, it leaves sediment that builds up over time. This area is called a delta. Rivers divide up into many channels as they cross deltas. Deltas are so-called because they are often triangular, like Delta, or ?, a letter of the Greek alphabet.

Delta shapes

Some deltas look like an arc; others look like the fingers of a hand, or like a bird's foot. Some deltas are very wide, stretching for hundreds of kilometres.

Deltas form when a river slows down to meet the sea. The sediment it carries drops to the bottom and along its banks. As the sediment builds up, the river cuts streams in it.

Fact file

Delta sizes

• The biggest delta in the world is formed by two great rivers, the Ganges and the Brahmaputra, in Bangladesh.
• Swamps on the Mississippi Delta (right) are shrinking every year, because there is less soil and sediment in the water.

▶ Salt water marshes and low islands in the Mississippi Delta.

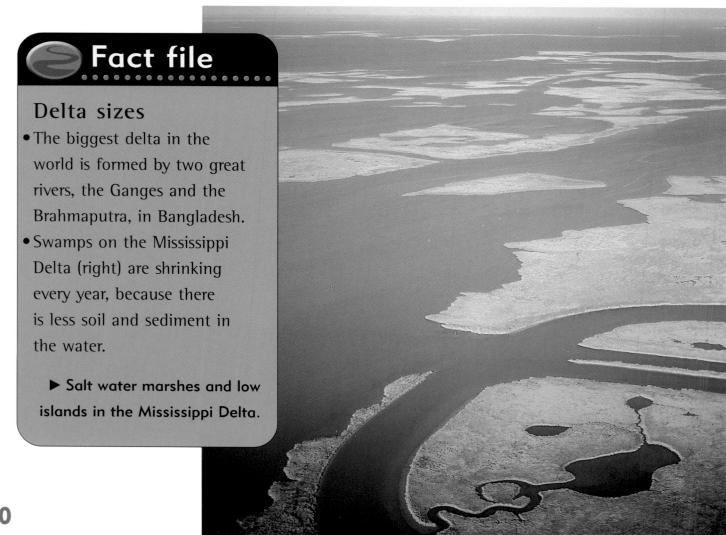

Low-lying islands

Over many thousands of years, sediment can build up. Plants take root in the mud. Their roots stop the mud from being washed away. Gradually, the mud changes into soil, and low, flat islands form in the river.

Low land in a delta often floods when the water level is high, or when storms send waves crashing in from the sea. But people often live and farm there, because the land is good for crops. In 1990, 140,000 people were killed by floods in the Ganges Delta.

Location file

The Sundarbans

In the River Ganges Delta, there are over 50 low islands, called the Sundarbans. The Sundarbans have the largest area of **mangrove** trees in the world. Mangrove trees are like trees that grow on stilts. Many rare animals live in this special habitat, including Bengal tigers, crocodiles and golden eagles.

▲ A fishing village in the Sundarbans, West Bengal, India.

▶ Rare Bengal tigers live in the mangrove swamps in the Sundarbans.

River wildlife

Rivers are home to fish, birds, insects and other animals. Fish feed on small animals and plants. Fish are food for birds, reptiles and mammals – including people.

Variety of life

An amazing range of animals lives in tropical rivers. The River Plata in South America has fish, caimans (a type of crocodile), water snakes, frogs, toads and crabs. Birds come to catch fish. Even in the coldest places, rivers are full of life. The icy River Ob in Siberia has over 50 types of fish.

In Africa, animals such as elephants and lions come to the river bank to drink. Animals may also eat the plants growing by the river, catch fish or hunt other animals that come to drink.

▼ **A pride of lions drinks by a river bank.**

Beavers

Beavers live beside rivers and lakes, mostly in North America. They build **dams** to make small lakes where they can live in safety. Beaver dams can block the flow of rivers and streams.

▶ **A beaver gnawing at a tree.**

Food chains

In the wild, each living thing is food for another living thing. This is called the food chain. Plants are at the bottom of the chain and hunting animals are at the top. So grass is eaten by ducks, who are eaten by foxes.

If one part of the food chain is harmed, other animals in the chain suffer. If fish are poisoned, animals that eat fish can be poisoned too.

 Fact file

Amazing salmon

• Salmon breed in rivers. The young salmon then swim out to sea, but return as adults. They often travel thousands of miles to swim back up the river where they hatched.
• Salmon can tell a particular river by its smell.

▼ **A grizzly bear catches a salmon as it leaps up a waterfall.**

Harvesting the river

Since ancient times people have gathered fish, plants and even ice from rivers. Today, fish farms are being built along rivers.

All around the world, people make a living from rivers. On the River Yenisey in Siberia, local people catch fish such as carp and perch, as well as sturgeon, the fish whose eggs are called caviar.

Food crops such as watercress are grown near rivers because they need lots of water. River plants such as reeds can be used for weaving or for roofs.

Fish farming

All over the world, too many wild fish are caught every year, and the number of wild fish left in rivers is falling. This has led to the opening of many fish farms.

▼ Fishermen set their nets at the edge of the River Yenisey in Siberia, Russia. The Yenisey has more than 30 types of fish.

Fish farms breed fish that are sold for food. This means that there are always enough fish, and so people can leave wild fish alone.

Fact file

World fish farming figures

- Fish from fish farms now account for nearly 50 per cent of the fish we eat.
- Fish farming produced 59.4 million tonnes of fish in 2004.
- Almost 70 per cent of the fish grown in fish farms comes from China.

▼ China has a long history of fish farming. Baby fish (fry) are raised in ponds next to the river. When they get big enough, the fish are put into the river.

Location file

Peru, South America

Local people in Pucullpa, a poor area of Peru, are trying to make small fish farms in ponds dug beside the Amazon. Pig or chicken waste is dropped in the water, which helps water plants grow. The fish feed on these plants. The fish farmers can either eat the fish or sell them to make money.

There are fish farms in seas, lakes, **reservoirs** and rivers. Many types of fish are grown and harvested in river fish farms. There are even alligator farms in the rivers of hot and tropical areas.

Protecting rivers

Rivers are fragile. They are polluted when chemicals are poured into them. Building on or near riverbanks makes it harder for animals to live there.

Most people's drinking water comes from rivers and reservoirs. In rich countries, water is cleaned before it comes out of the tap. In many poor countries, people have to drink and wash in a river. Millions of people all over the world have no clean water to drink. Dirty water can cause diseases.

▼ A woman in Nepal has to wash her pots in a polluted river.

Fact file

Pollution accidents
- In 2000, poisoned water spilled out of an old mine in Romania into the rivers Szamos and Tisza. All living creatures were killed along a 400-km stretch of the river.
- Thousands of animals were killed in the Guadiamar River in Spain in 1998 when poisonous mud spilled into a river after a reservoir broke its banks.

The grandmother of the Glades

Marjory Stoneman Douglas (1890-1998) spent her life trying to protect wildlife. In 1947 her book *River of Grass* began a campaign to protect mangrove swamps in the Mississippi Delta. In 1993, aged 103, she was awarded a Presidential Medal.

▲ Marjory Stoneman Douglas checks a grass stalk.

Pollution

Rivers can become polluted in many ways. Waste from factories is poured into them. Chemicals used in farming wash off the soil and into a river. Old lead, coal and tin mines are also a problem. The mining tunnels fill up with water, which is polluted by the metal and rusty machinery. The dirty water ends up in a river.

River civilizations

The earliest civilizations grew up near rivers in Egypt, India and China. Rivers provided water and people could travel along them.

First cities

The world's first cities grew up in Mesopotamia, in the Middle East. The name Mesopotamia in Greek means 'the land between two rivers'. These two rivers, the Tigris and the Euphrates, flooded their banks every spring. The floods left a rich layer of mud which was good for planting crops. The people had plenty of food, and the cities grew.

The people of ancient Egypt also depended on the flooding of the River Nile.

Early farming

The farmers of Mesopotamia and ancient Egypt built many ditches, **canals** and reservoirs to bring water to their crops. They grew food crops and flax (a type of plant). Flax was woven to make linen for clothing, sails and ropes. In Egypt, papyrus was grown to make a type of paper.

▼ A farm worker with a modern water pump in Egypt. The water comes from the Nile.

Sacred rivers

Rivers are so important to people
that they are considered holy by many
religions. They often represent a
connection between life and death,
or sometimes their flow represents
the eternal flow of life.

Boats and waterwheels

Rivers have been used since ancient times for transport and as a source of power. People have now found better ways of using rivers.

Improving rivers

Many rivers have been changed to make them safe for large ships. The River Rhine in Germany has been dug deeper so boats can sail on it for over 800 km. Meanders on the Mississippi River in the USA have been straightened to let larger boats pass.

When a river drops too steeply for boats, one answer is to build a lock and weir. A weir is a small step built across the river, and a lock is a small enclosure where the water level can be raised or lowered.

 Fact file

China's waterways
- China has over 100,000 km of canals and rivers that boats can sail on.
- China's Grand Canal is the longest canal in the world. It was begun over 2,400 years ago.
- On the Yangtze and Wu Rivers, steel cables pull boats safely over dangerous rapids.

▲ The Mississippi River is so big that dozens of barges can be herded together and floated downriver.

Benoit Fourneyron

In 1827 a young Frenchman, Benoit Fourneyron, invented the water **turbine**, a smaller and better type of waterwheel. During Fourneyron's lifetime, scientists laughed at his invention. However, in 1895, 30 years after Fourneyron died, turbines were installed at Niagara Falls to make electricity. Turbines are still used today.

Water power

River power has been used since Roman times, when mills with wooden waterwheels were built beside rivers. These mills did many things, such as grinding grain for flour. In the nineteenth century, waterwheels powered factory machines, such as **looms**. In the twentieth century, people started using water power to make electricity.

▶ This waterwheel was built in the nineteenth century to power a sawmill in Sherbrooke, Canada.

Crossing the river

A river forms a natural barrier. Crossing a river safely is quite a challenge. Through the ages, new ways of crossing rivers have been invented.

The simplest way of crossing a stream or small river is to wade through at a shallow point, called a ford. Villages that grew up at crossing points have names such as Bedford or Stratford.

The first bridges were built out of stone, wood or ropes. The Romans were the first to build arched bridges. The first metal bridge was built in 1779, over the River Severn at Ironbridge, in the UK.

Over the past 200 years, new kinds of bridges have been built. They are often made out of steel or **concrete**.

Fact file

Bridge facts

- The Runyang Bridge across the mouth of the Yangtze River, in China, is the longest river crossing in the world. It is 23 km long.
- The Gateshead Millennium Bridge (below) over the River Tyne in England, opened in 2001. It is known as the 'blinking eye' bridge because it looks like an eyelid blinking when it tips up to let ships pass underneath.
- There are no bridges at all across the River Amazon. It is too wide. When the Amazon floods, it can become 48 km wide!

▼ The Gateshead Millennium Bridge tips up to allow ships to pass under it.

▲ The Jiangyin Bridge over the River Yangtze is the world's second-longest cable-suspended river bridge, after the Humber Bridge in the UK.

Tunnels and ferries

Tunnelling is another way to cross a river. The first tunnel under the River Thames in London, UK, was completed in 1843. In 2007, two double-decker road tunnels under the River Seine in France will be completed, eight years after work began.

Ferries also cross rivers. They range from simple rowing boats to double- or triple-decker ships.

◄ Some ferries are simple boats, like this one on the Meghna River, Bangladesh.

Dams and reservoirs

A river provides drinking water, but the amount of water in a river can change. A **dam** is a way of storing water. Today dams can provide energy too.

A dam is a wall across a river which holds the water back. The Nurek Dam on the River Vakhsh in Tajikistan is the highest dam in the world.

When a dam is built, the water rises behind it to fill the river valley. It forms a lake, called a reservoir. Water is then let out gradually, through drains built in the dam.

Three Gorges Dam
The Three Gorges Dam on the Yangtze River, in China, will be the largest **hydroelectric** dam in the world – over 1 km across, creating a 560 km reservoir. Despite protests from local people, the dam was begun in 1994 and will be finished in 2009.

▼ This diagram shows how a dam works.

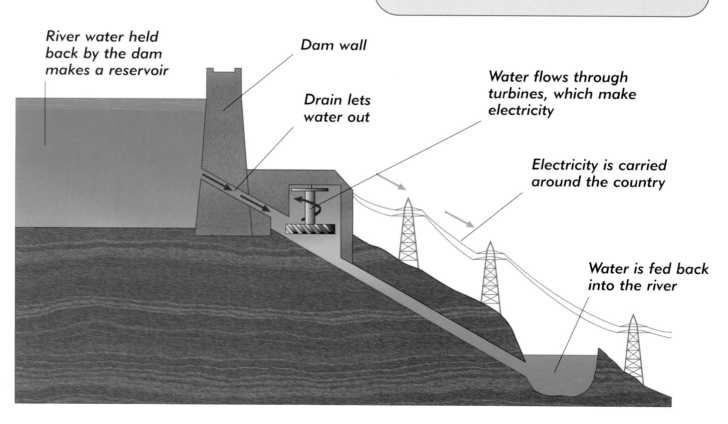

River water held back by the dam makes a reservoir

Dam wall

Drain lets water out

Water flows through turbines, which make electricity

Electricity is carried around the country

Water is fed back into the river

Hydroelectricity

The power of water flowing out through a dam can be used to make electricity, known as hydroelectricity. As the water flows, it turns turbines in the dam's drains, which make electricity. The Hoover Dam on the Colorado River in the USA was completed in 1936. It was one of the first hydroelectric dams.

Hydroelectric dams are very expensive to build. The electricity may cost too much for ordinary local people. The rising water drowns towns in the valley. Thousands of people can lose their homes.

▲ The Glen Canyon Dam in Utah, USA, was finished in 1963. It changed the flow of the Colorado River and affected wildlife along it.

Fact file

Dam disasters

- A flash flood in 1889 in Pennsylvania, USA, broke a dam. Two thousand people were killed in an hour.
- In 1963, a landslide fell into the Vaiont Dam reservoir in Italy. A huge wave shot out of the reservoir and killed 3,000 people. The dam was not seriously damaged.

Estuary energy

Some river estuaries offer a new source of energy: tidal energy. In an estuary, sea water flows in and out with the tides. Tides can be used to make energy.

Tide mills

Tidal energy has been used for centuries. Beginning in the eleventh century, tide mills were built on river estuaries in Europe. Most mills were used for grinding grain. Centuries later, tide mills were built on river estuaries in the USA and in Guyana, South America. They were used to crush sugar cane.

▼ A traditional tidal mill on the River Rance, in France, at low tide.

 **Fact file**

Energy from nature

- In 2001, only 6% of the USA's energy came from the sun, water and wind.
- Energy such as tidal energy is up to four times more expensive than energy from coal or gas. But energy from the sun, water and wind does not cause pollution and does not run out.

◀ River estuaries such as this one in Canada, with a big difference between low and high tide, are the best places for tidal power stations.

Tidal energy

More recently, tidal power stations have been built or planned on river estuaries around the world. The best places are where there is a big difference between high and low tide. At the Bay of Fundy in Canada, the difference can be up to 20 m, the most in the world.

The Cardiff Bay Barrage in Wales could be used to make tidal energy. However, estuary mudflats are important for many birds and animals who feed and raise their babies there. Building tidal power stations could harm wildlife, so only a few tidal power stations have been built so far.

Location file

La Rance power station

The tidal power station at La Rance, France (right), opened in 1966. A barrier stretches across the estuary of the River Rance. Water flows through the barrier and turns turbines which make electricity for a million homes.

▶ La Rance estuary power station.

Rivers in flood

When a river floods, the water can spread very quickly over the land. Some rivers flood every year. Other floods are unexpected disasters.

Most floods happen when there is heavy rain or when a lot of snow melts. If the ground is already wet, the extra water runs straight into rivers, which then flood. High tides from the sea can also cause flooding.

Flood disasters are very dangerous, sometimes killing thousands of people. The rushing water damages homes, factories and farms. Roads and railways can be swept away. When the Mississippi flooded in 1993, 30,000 homes were damaged. The Yellow River is also known as 'China's Sorrow'. It has caused some of the worst natural disasters ever.

Location file

The River Arno flood

The city of Florence, in Italy, is famous for its art and architecture. In November 1966, the River Arno flooded to its highest level for 600 years. More than 1,000 paintings, 300,000 rare books and 700,000 historic documents were soaked or covered in black, smelly slime. It took many years to repair the damage.

◄ People on a raft in a flooded street of Florence, during the flood of 1966.

Getting worse

In many parts of the world, floods are getting worse. This is because people are cutting down forests, and building more homes, roads and paved areas. These buildings make it harder for water to soak into the ground. In cities, drains carry the extra water quickly into the rivers, much quicker than in nature. Homes are built in areas that have been known to flood.

▲ People in Mozambican floods in 2000 wait on a rooftop to be rescued.

 Fact file

River flood disasters

The four worst river flood disasters in recorded history have all been on two rivers in China, the Yellow River and the Yangtze River. A major flood on the Yellow River in 1887 killed around a million people. The Yangtze River killed 140,000 people when it flooded in 1931.

Flood defences

Floods are dangerous, but flood defences can help. Some flood defences are expensive, but there are cheaper ways to protect people who live near rivers.

Levees

One way of preventing floods is to build a levee. A levee is a wall on top of the banks of the river. Levees stop water from spilling over the top when the water level is high. Levees can be made higher with sandbags, rocks and soil. However, they can make floods worse downstream.

▲ Levees along the River Garonne in France protect the city of Toulouse from flooding.

Location file

The Thames Barrier

The River Thames flows through London, and for years flooding was a problem. A large flood barrier (below) was completed in 1982. It has ten separate gates that can be closed when there is danger of a flood. This type of flood defence works, but it costs a lot to build.

▼ The Thames Barrier in London, UK.

Dredging

Another way of preventing floods is to clear, or **dredge**, riverbeds. This means scooping out sediment that has settled on the bottom, clogging the river up.

Planting

Planting trees near rivers helps too. Trees soak up water from the ground, so less water runs into rivers. Roots stop soil from washing away and clogging up rivers.

Safer building

People often build houses in low areas which can flood. Building homes on higher ground is safer.

▲ Dredging a harbour in Germany. Dredging makes the riverbed deeper so that large ships can sail on it.

 **Fact file**

Levees

- In ancient Egypt, 960 km of levees were built along the west bank of the River Nile.
- Levees were first built on the banks of the Mississippi River, USA, in the 1700s.
- In 2005 a powerful hurricane named Katrina hit New Orleans, USA. The levees were broken on the Mississippi River and four-fifths of the city was flooded. More than 1,300 people died in the disaster.

Enjoying rivers

Rivers are great places to relax. People walk, fish and camp near rivers. River sports are becoming more popular. The number of tourists is growing, but tourism can cause problems for wildlife.

Fishing

Fishing is an ancient sport. The Chinese were fishing with a silk line 2,400 years ago. In many countries today, fishing is the most popular sport. As fishing is now limited on rivers to protect wild fish, people often go fishing on **artificial** lakes.

Some people think fishing is a cruel sport. Fishing lines, lead weights and nets can harm birds and fish if they are left in the water.

Location file

River Sjoa, Norway

Norway's River Sjoa is a popular tourist attraction. High in the mountains, holidaymakers can try out potholing, fishing and mountaineering as well as whitewater rafting.

▼ An American whitewater rafting team rows along the Zambezi River in Africa.

▲ Families enjoy a beach on the
River Rhine in Germany.

New river sports

Canoeing, or kayaking, became
a popular sport in the nineteenth
century. Whitewater canoeing is
a sport where canoes travel through
gates, rapids and waterfalls in a river.
New river sports are being invented
all the time.

Travel agencies offer whitewater
rafting activity holidays in wild and
beautiful surroundings, on rivers such
as the Zambezi in Africa. Tourism is
good for local businesses, but it can
also damage nature. Too many
tourists can ruin the place they have
come so far to see.

 Fact file

River tourism around the world

- Turkey's government is encouraging river
  sports on the River Göksu, but also
  protecting the birds that live there.
- In 2002, Cambodia, Laos and Vietnam
  built piers, walking trails and information
  centres all along the Mekong River.
- The government of Botswana, in
  southern Africa, is promoting tourism
  on the Chobe River that will not hurt
  its wildlife.

43

Rivers for life

As more and more people need fresh water for industry, farms and homes, we need to make sure that we use water more carefully.

Using water

In the world's richest countries, each person uses twenty times more water than people in the poorest countries. Farms use more water to grow luxury crops, such as flowers. This means more and more water is taken from rivers.

If too much water is taken from a river, it can run dry. People living downstream may not have enough water, and the water left may become polluted. Many rivers around the world are running dry. Part of China's Yellow River ran dry for seven months in 1997.

The Yellow River, in China, ran dry in 1997.

▶ A child drinks clean water from a tap installed by the charity WaterAid. WaterAid brings safe water to the world's poorest people.

Water in war – and peace

Water is so important that it can be a target during war. During many wars in the twentieth century, dams were bombed on purpose. This left people without water and caused flooding.

Water wars may happen in the future where different groups want the same water. Many countries are trying to share river water. The River Zambezi is used by six countries in Africa. Some of these countries have agreed to share water more fairly.

Glossary

Artificial Made by people.

Barge A flat-bottomed boat used on rivers and canals to carry goods.

Bed The bottom of a river.

Canal A narrow waterway made to bring water to crops or for boats to travel along.

Concrete A mixture of cement and gravel that becomes hard when dry.

Dam A wall built across a river or stream to hold back water.

Delta A place where a river divides up into many streams as it reaches the sea.

Dredge To scoop soil and sediment from the bottom of a river to deepen or clear it.

Estuary The wide part of a river, where it meets the sea.

Evaporation When water is turned into an invisible vapour in the air.

Flash flood A sudden flood.

Glacier A huge river of ice.

Habitat The place where an animal needs to live.

Hydroelectric Electricity made using flowing water.

Loom A machine that makes cloth.

Mangrove A tropical tree with special roots that grows in salty coastal water.

Meander The loops and curves made by a slow-moving river.

Middle Ages The time in history between the fifth century and the fifteenth century.

Mouth The place where a river meets the sea.

Mudflats The muddy area at the mouth of a river when the tide is out.

Rapids Part of a river where the water flows and swirls down rocks.

Reservoir An artificial lake for storing water.

Sediment Little bits of rocks and soil that are carried by a river.

Source The origin or head of a river.

Spring A source, where water comes out of rock.

Tropical An area on the Earth, near the Equator, that is warm.

Turbine A spinning motor that makes electricity.

Further information

▲ The Golden Gate Bridge links San Francisco and the Marin Peninsula in California, USA. It was completed in 1937.

Websites to visit

www.wateraid.org.uk
WaterAid is an international charity that provides clean water and advice to the world's poorest people.

www.wonderquest.com/Meanders.htm
This webpage explains in detail how meanders form in slow-flowing rivers.

www.bbc.co.uk/schools/riversandcoasts/rivers/change_river/index.shtml
User-friendly website that shows how rivers form and change and what happens when they meet the sea, with printable worksheets.

www.ncwildlife.org/pg10_OutdoorKids/pg10b5a.htm
The children's page on the North Carolina Wildlife Resources Commission website explains a lot of difficult terms to do with rivers.

Books to read

Our World: Rivers and Lakes by Kate Bedford, (Franklin Watts, 2006)

Earth's Changing Landscape: Rivers in Action by Mary Green (Smart Apple Media, 2004)

Rivers Through Time: Settlements of the Indus River by Rob Bowden (Heinemann Library, 2006)

Index

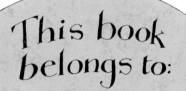

This book
belongs to:

Heather Brown

TO DEAR PAT TUPPER AND ALL THE FAMILY
WITH TONS OF LOVE AS EVER

First American edition, 1989.
Text and illustrations copyright © 1989 by Jill Murphy.
All rights reserved.
Originated and published in Great Britain by Walker Books Ltd.
Printed in Italy.
Library of Congress Cataloging-in-Publication Data
Murphy, Jill. p. cm.
Summary: When Mama Elephant puts her family on a diet,
their will power remains strong until Granny sends a cake.
[1. Weight control – Fiction.   2. Size – Fiction.
3. Elephants – Fiction.] I. Title.
PZ7.M9534Pi 1989 [E] – dc19 89-3639 CIP AC
ISBN 0-399-21590-5
G.P. Putnam's Sons, 200 Madison Avenue, NYC 10016
1 3 5 7 9 10 8 6 4 2
First impression

A Piece of Cake

Jill Murphy

G. P. Putnam's Sons   New York

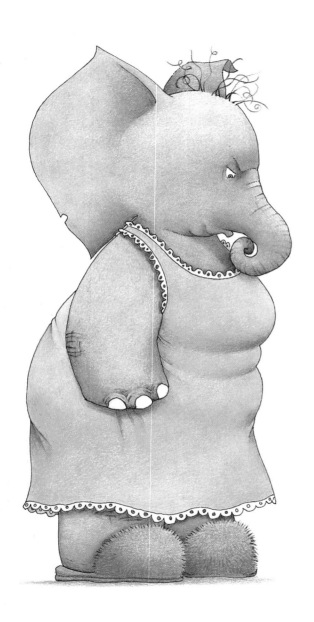

"I'm fat," said Mrs. Large.

"No you're not," said Lester.

"You're our cuddly mommy,"
said Laura.

"You're *just* right," said Luke.

"Mommy's got wobbly bits,"
said the baby.

"Exactly," said Mrs. Large. "As I was
saying – I'm fat."

"We must all go on a diet," said Mrs. Large. "No more cake. No more cookies. No more potato chips. No more sitting around all day. From now on, it's healthy living."

"Can we watch TV?" asked Lester, as they trooped in from school.

"Certainly not!" said Mrs. Large. "We're all off for a nice healthy jog around the park."

And they were.

"What's our snack, Mom?" asked Laura
when they arrived home.

"Some nice healthy watercress soup," said
Mrs. Large. "Followed by a nice healthy cup
of water."

"Oh!" said Laura. "That sounds . . . nice."

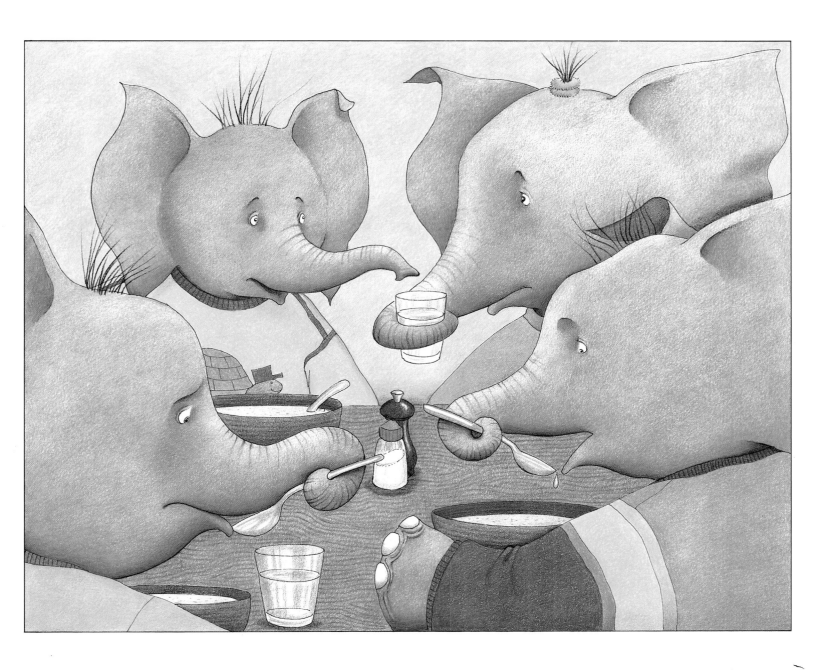

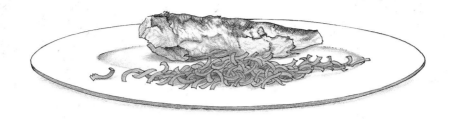

"I'm just going to watch the news, dear,"
said Mr. Large when he came home from work.
"No you're not, dear," said Mrs. Large.
"You're off for a nice healthy jog around
the park, followed by supper – delicious
fish with grated carrots."
"I can't wait," said Mr. Large.

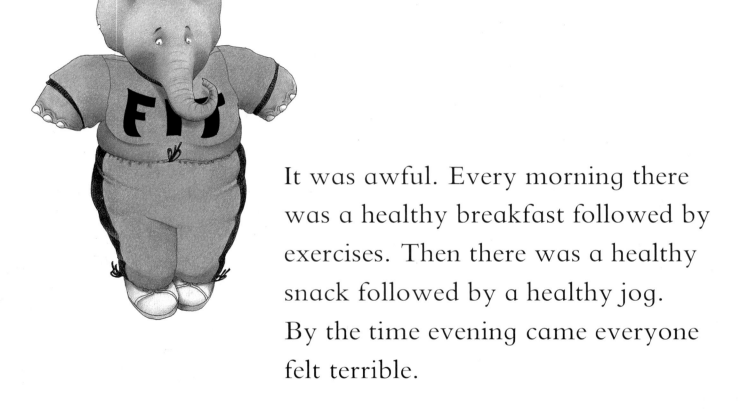

It was awful. Every morning there was a healthy breakfast followed by exercises. Then there was a healthy snack followed by a healthy jog. By the time evening came everyone felt terrible.

"We aren't getting any thinner, dear,"
said Mr. Large.

"Perhaps elephants are *meant* to be fat,"
said Luke.

"Nonsense!" said Mrs. Large. "We mustn't
give up now."

"Wibbly wobbly wibbly wobbly," went
the baby.

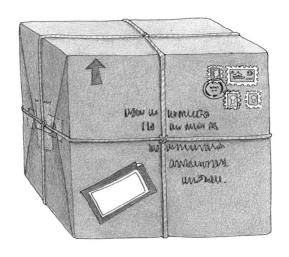

One morning a parcel arrived. It was a cake from Granny. Everyone stared at it hopefully. Mrs. Large put it into the cupboard on a high shelf. "Just in case we have visitors," she said sternly.

Everyone kept thinking about the cake.
They thought about it during the healthy jog.
They thought about it during supper.
They thought about it in bed that
night. Mrs. Large sat up. "I can't stand
it anymore," she said to herself. "I must
have a piece of that cake."

Mrs. Large crept out of bed and went downstairs to the kitchen. She took a knife out of the drawer and opened the cupboard. There was only one piece of cake left!

"Ah ha!" said Mr. Large, seeing the knife.
"Caught in the act!"
Mrs. Large switched on the light and saw
Mr. Large and all the children hiding
under the table.
"There *is* one piece left," said Laura in
a helpful way.

Mrs. Large began to laugh. "We're all as bad as each other!" she said, eating the last piece of cake before anyone else did.

"I do think elephants are meant to be fat," said Luke.

"I think you're probably right, dear," said Mrs. Large.

"Wibbly wobbly wibbly wobbly!" went the baby.